Doulton transfer-decorated Lambeth Combination flush-out closet.

Ceramic Water Closets

Munroe Blair

A Shire Book

Published in 2000 by Shire Publications Ltd, Cromwell
House, Church Street, Princes Risborough,
Buckinghamshire HP27 9AA, UK.
(Website: www.shirebooks.co.uk)

British Library Cataloguing in Publication Data:
Blair, Munroe
Ceramic water closets. – (The Shire book)
1. Toilets – Great Britain – History – 19th century
2. Toilets – Great Britain – History – 20th century
3. Ceramic industries – Great Britain
I. Title 696.1'82'0941'09
ISBN 0 7478 0457 5

Cover: *Thomas Twyford's Twycliffe hand-enamelled syphon-jet closet, with bracket-supported mahogany seat and cover.*

ACKNOWLEDGEMENTS
The accuracy of information contained in this book could not have been achieved without
the help and guidance of many people with specific expertise in various aspects of the
subject. The author is indebted to those who contributed towards ensuring the historical
accuracy of water-closet development. Space does not permit naming all those who so
willingly gave their time and advice. Everyone's help was sincerely appreciated; thank you
all. The extensive help extended to the author by the following individuals and organisa-
tions deserves special mention: Terry Woolliscroft, Caradon Plumbing Solutions, for
archive research and photographic help; Angela Lee, Gladstone Working Pottery Museum,
for her unlimited patience during photographic and research sessions; Roger Cooper, Ideal-
Standard; David Woodcock, the National Museum of Science and Industry; Julie
McKeown, Sir Henry Doulton Gallery/Royal Doulton; Ruth Brown, Staffordshire Univer-
sity Slide Library; Miranda Goodby, Potteries Museum and Art Gallery; Luitwin Gisberg
von Boch-Galhau, Villeroy & Boch; Gaye Blake Roberts and the dedicated Wedgwood
Museum team; Sam Woodberry, Armitage Shanks.

Printed in Great Britain by CIT Printing Services Ltd,
Press Buildings, Merlins Bridge, Haverfordwest,
Pembrokeshire SA61 1XF.

Contents

Note: for ease of reference, terms and names that are explained in the glossary are printed in italic type when they first occur in the text.

Early water closets

Sir John Harington, a godson of Queen Elizabeth I, designed the first water closet in 1592, the *Ajax*. It so impressed Elizabeth that she ordered one for Richmond Palace. Except for a water-sealed outlet trap, Harington's sixteenth-century closet included most features of a late-twentieth-century WC. Ancient Roman plumbing in Bath, 4 miles (6 km) away from Harington's home at Kelston, was the likely inspiration for his WC design. The published cost of the Ajax was 30s 8d. This price would have exceeded the annual income of a contemporary farm labourer. Two centuries later WCs remained expensive and could be afforded only by the very wealthy.

The *privy* of the seventeenth-century diarist Samuel Pepys discharged into a cesspit in his cellar. Pepys recorded how his cesspit was manually emptied in buckets carried through the house. By the end of the eighteenth century valve-type WCs were popular with the wealthy, but they invariably discharged into cesspits rather than drains. In city homes these cesspits were occasionally outside buildings but the majority were in domestic cellars. The emptying arrangements available to Pepys still existed in early Victorian times, the service being carried out by nightsoil men.

Water closets installed in the eighteenth-century homes of wealthy families were flushed by valves or cisterns. However, mains water was

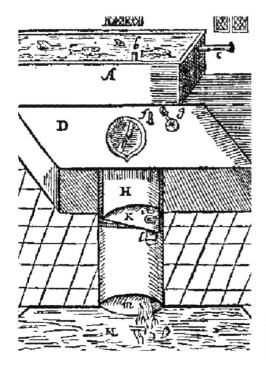

Sir John Harington's sixteenth-century WC, the 'Ajax'. It included most of the features of a modern WC: cistern, flushing handle, bowl and outlet.

This commode conceals a pottery jerry pot and lid. It was emptied manually.

not always available to cleanse these early closets. During the eighteenth century piped mains water had been introduced in some cities but supplies were unreliable. Most mains water flowed only for one or two hours on two or three days of the week. Water pressure and flow rates varied and supplies were at best intermittent. Filling storage tanks in the roof space required the manual opening of a mains *watercock* control valve at appropriate times. In 1748 ball valves replaced the chore of controlling water flow into storage tanks to serve household needs by gravity. Availability of piped water led to increasing numbers of WCs, which in turn led to intolerable demands on overloaded disposal systems.

Ashpit or privy closet. The contents were covered with ashes before being cleared manually by nightsoil men.

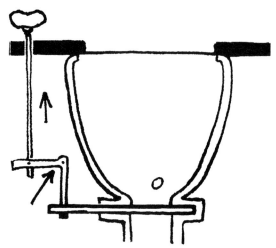

Alexander Cummings's patented WC of 1775 with the slider valve outlet and low inlet to create a cleansing water swirl inside the bowl.

Metal valve closets

Alexander Cummings, a London watchmaker, registered the first water-closet patent in 1775. Cummings's WC had a slider valve to close the outlet hole from cesspit odours. Operation of the outlet valve simultaneously opened a watercock intended to create a cleansing water swirl inside the bowl. Unfortunately, rust often impaired the effective operation of Cummings's sliding outlet plate, but failure to open the valve did not deter householders from using the closet until it overflowed. Rather than improve the faulty valve's operation, water-sealed overflows were added to bypass blockages. Overflow arrangements remained a feature of *valve closets* for nearly two hundred years.

Joseph Bramah, a locksmith, engineer and inventor, adapted Cummings's idea in 1778, replacing the slider with a self-cleansing

Joseph Bramah's 1778 WC, with a hinged valve enclosed within the outlet chamber below the metal bowl. The trapped over-flow from the bowl bypassed the outlet valve to prevent overspilling.

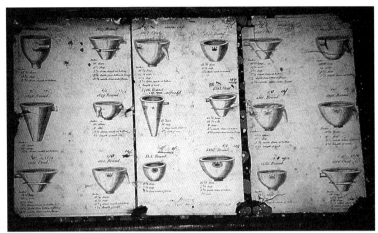

hinged outlet valve. Bramah's design, with its effective outlet seal, became more popular than that of Cummings. The hinged seal was designed to hold water in the bowl and stop cesspit gas entering the dwelling it served. The introduction of Bramah's improved valve closet came almost two hundred years after Harington's original WC idea. Within twenty years of his patent Bramah claimed sales of six thousand valve-type WCs.

Early metal valve closets were operated by cumbersome metal workings concealed in wooden cabinets. They suffered from constant malfunction, adding to the health hazard they were intended to prevent. Valve-closet manufacturers co-ordinated component supplies and their assembly, but sanitary progress was slow and their basic design remained unchanged for a further hundred years. Problems included the likelihood of flushing water spilling over and customer dissatisfaction with the bowl's painted cast-iron finish. A commercial opportunity to replace metal bowls with ceramic alternatives gave pioneer sanitary potters the incentive to improve WC design.

Josiah Wedgwood, the celebrated English ceramist, recorded making a pottery 'close stool water closet' pan' in April 1777. Often referred to as the 'father of English industrial pottery', Wedgwood made pans to the WC design drawing of an inventor, Richard Edgeworth, and produced bowls for several closet manufacturers, including Joseph Bramah.

Pottery bowls were requested with flanges to sit into metal valve discharge boxes. Rims to contain spillage were incorporated and holes to secure copper flushing spreader plates. Rust-prone cast iron was eventually replaced by glazed ceramic bowls with *returned* or *full flushing rims*. Ceramic bowls were easier to clean, lighter in weight, not liable to corrosion and much cheaper than their metal predecessors. The main mechanical parts of valve closets continued to be made in either cast iron or copper with brass water valves.

Twyford 1809 earthenware pan closet bowl, transfer-decorated with a classical landscape. The copper 'flushing spreader plate' bolted under the return rim was designed to spread a cleansing film of water around the bowl. The cast-iron supporting container enclosed a pivoted pan to retain a water seal.

Pottery valve-closet bowl with overflow holes and side supply spigot to direct a spiral of cleansing water around the flushing rim. The underside view (below) shows a turned-down spigot to bypass any outlet-valve blockage and a metal flange for fixing to the cast-iron valve discharge casing.

The development of pottery water closets

Early pottery pan and trap WC developed from the metal stink-trap. A U-bend divides the WC sump below the water level to prevent sewer gas entering dwellings.

Pottery bowls were easily made with features such as overflow *spigots* to bypass faulty outlet valves. Potters received only a few shillings for their bowls, but valve-closet manufacturers charged high prices for complete closets. Valve-closet manufacturers often supplied assemblies complete with cabinets and installed them in dwellings. When flushing directly from mains water a closet was considered 'plumbed-in' or a 'fixture'. In 1782 John Gaittait patented a *stink-trap* designed to close out cesspit odours. These *water-sealed traps,* recognised today as U-bends, were adopted as a key element of closet design. Traps were expensive to fabricate in metal but easily made in pottery. With the ease of production in their favour, pottery WCs were poised to challenge the monopoly held by metal valve closets.

Potters now began to question the need for outlet valves when water-sealed traps proved more effective. To gain a larger share of the WC market, it was essential for potters to break free of the valve-closet makers. With the help of plumbers and sanitary engineers, potters took a more active role in WC bowl design. Overflows that had been essential safeguards against malfunctioning valve outlets were unnecessary on pottery WCs that had the advantage of self-cleansing traps.

However, although noisy and less hygienic, valve closets, when enclosed in mahogany cabinets, were more attractive than the simple pottery bowl and trap WCs. Sales of pottery WCs remained poor despite their superior flushing performance. Potters gained extensive flushing experience by making simple closets that had a pan with a supporting water-sealed trap for the growing cheaper end of the market. These WCs needed no outlet

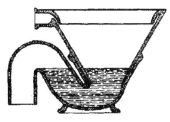

THOMAS TWYFORD, HANLEY,
STAFFORDSHIRE.

VALVE, SHIP, AND PORTABLE CLOSET BASINS.

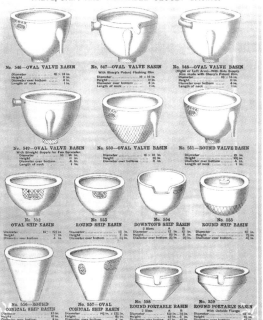

Page from a Twyford catalogue showing valve-closet basins.

9

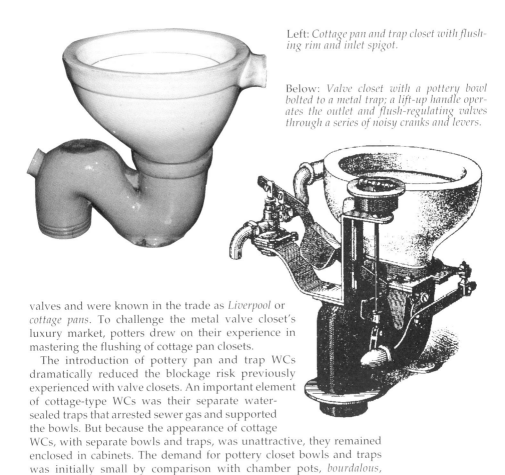

Left: *Cottage pan and trap closet with flushing rim and inlet spigot.*

Below: *Valve closet with a pottery bowl bolted to a metal trap; a lift-up handle operates the outlet and flush-regulating valves through a series of noisy cranks and levers.*

valves and were known in the trade as *Liverpool* or *cottage pans*. To challenge the metal valve closet's luxury market, potters drew on their experience in mastering the flushing of cottage pan closets.

The introduction of pottery pan and trap WCs dramatically reduced the blockage risk previously experienced with valve closets. An important element of cottage-type WCs was their separate water-sealed traps that arrested sewer gas and supported the bowls. But because the appearance of cottage WCs, with separate bowls and traps, was unattractive, they remained enclosed in cabinets. The demand for pottery closet bowls and traps was initially small by comparison with chamber pots, *bourdalous*, washing bowls or water-jug sets. However, potters realised that here was a potential new market.

Wedgwood's 1830 coach pot, or bourdalou, with transfer-printed Capriccio landscape decoration. This pattern is recorded in Wedgwood's 1802 drawing book but was made from the 1770s to the 1860s.

Sir Henry Doulton,
1820–97, Victorian
pottery manufacturer
and sanitary engineer.

Sewers and the pottery industry

During the industrial revolution of the eighteenth and nineteenth centuries agricultural populations moved into industrial areas and cities seeking work. In these expanding conurbations drinking water was polluted and sewage disposal systems were inadequate or non-existent. Increased discharge of untreated sewage rapidly overwhelmed natural rivers and waterways, reducing them to choked open sewers. In 1832 drinking water drawn from London's contaminated rivers was responsible for the first of several horrific cholera epidemics. In 1840 John Snow, who became anaesthetist to Queen Victoria, linked cholera and typhoid fever with contaminated water supplies. Inefficient drains exacerbated the situation, with cholera and typhoid claiming the lives of 29,000 Londoners between 1832 and 1866. During the same period over 50,000 lives were lost to cholera throughout Britain.

In common with cities around the world, mid-nineteenth-century London had no effective system of self-cleansing sewers. Repeated cholera outbreaks forced the government to take action. In 1848 the Public Health Act stated 'it shall not be lawful newly to erect, or to

11

rebuild any House, without a sufficient Water closet, Privy or Ashpit'. This was the first Health Act to make provision for sanitary facilities inside all new dwellings. Legislation alone could not beat cholera, but the Act started a national drive to provide efficient WC drainage systems.

Henry Doulton (1820–97) identified the commercial potential for drainage pipes to connect houses into London's anticipated new sewer system. The projected need for drainpipes encouraged Doulton, in 1846, to open a stoneware pipe factory at Lambeth in London.

Doulton made a vital contribution to public hygiene by realising the importance of pottery drainpipes. He was knighted in 1887. The following year he reflected on the appalling and insanitary conditions that had existed in 1850. He wrote in the 1888 *Sanitary Record*: 'pottery had then scarcely any use in connection with house sewerage or town drainage. . . . it is not too much to say that the manufacture and use of pottery has advanced side by side with engineering sanitary science.' Indeed, in addition to the established clay bricks, roofing tiles and tableware, by the twentieth century drainpipes, WCs, traps, baths and sinks had all become vital ceramic elements in British homes.

Although Henry Doulton built his drainpipe factory in London, Britain's industrial potteries were mainly located in North Staffordshire. Potting expertise was established in Staffordshire because of the local availability not only of clay, but also of long-flame coal for firing, and salt for glazing the ware. Staffordshire had a worldwide reputation for quality pottery, plus the skill to support the main concentration of industrial-scale sanitary pottery factories. WCs were the principal item that dictated the need to create a specialised sanitary pottery industry.

Twyford's stand at the 1901 Glasgow International Exhibition.

Pedestal water closets

By the middle of the nineteenth century water closets ceased to be regarded as a luxury but were seen as a necessity if urban disease was to be overcome. Ceramic bowl and trap WCs gradually began to dominate the volume market. Many well-known potters such as Copeland, Doulton, Edward Johns, Minton, Shanks, Twyford, Wedgwood and Enoch Wood were making pottery WC bowls, plug wash bowls, bidets and other toiletware. Amongst the most successful pioneers of sanitary pottery were the Twyford brothers, Christopher and Thomas. In 1848 Thomas Twyford (1827–72), an innovative, practical potter and sanitary engineer, committed his family's domestic pottery in Hanley to the exclusive manufacture of sanitaryware, including their specialised range of WCs.

The Great Exhibition of 1851 in London highlighted the lack of interest in free-standing, plumbed-in pottery WCs. The exhibition catalogue recorded only one pottery WC displayed, by John Ridgway of Shelton, Staffordshire. Pandering to Victorian taste in bathroom decor, John Ridgway's WC emulated in pottery the appearance of the popular mahogany closet cabinet. Internally Ridgway's design simply concealed a Bramah-style valve closet within a pottery shell. Ridgway's WC, and the public toilets introduced at the 1851 Exhibition, helped start the process of sanitary reform in Victorian Britain.

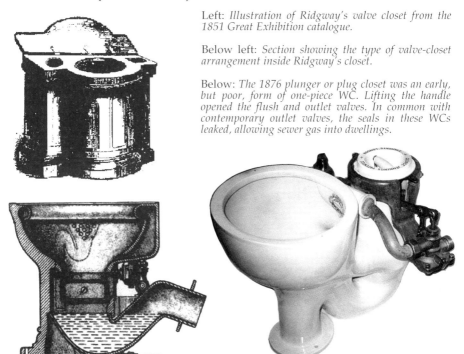

Left: *Illustration of Ridgway's valve closet from the 1851 Great Exhibition catalogue.*

Below left: *Section showing the type of valve-closet arrangement inside Ridgway's closet.*

Below: *The 1876 plunger or plug closet was an early, but poor, form of one-piece WC. Lifting the handle opened the flush and outlet valves. In common with contemporary outlet valves, the seals in these WCs leaked, allowing sewer gas into dwellings.*

Decorated white earthenware wash-out WC bowl supported on a pottery trap.

Although during the last quarter of the nineteenth century the majority of pottery WC bowls and water-sealed traps were still separate items, the idea of joining the two was being worked on. *Plunger* or *plug closets* were early attempts to join bowls and traps but were unsatisfactory for exposed installation. Potters knew that until they could supply WCs to satisfy Victorian aesthetic taste their pottery would remain concealed in cabinets. The challenge was to enclose the bowl and trap inside a pedestal to create free-standing WCs. Substantial potting expertise was therefore directed to the improvement and promotion of exposed pottery pedestal WCs. In addition, health-conscious authorities began to recommend the exposed water closets as they allowed access to possible faulty joints, thus facilitating speedy detection and repair.

Pottery water-sealed trap WCs had established their value by eliminating the need for expensive metal-valve outlet contraptions. Unlike valve closets, late-nineteenth-century pottery WCs were designed to be independent of wooden cabinets. The term 'valve' dropped out of use when pottery water-sealed traps replaced metal outlet arrangements. Efficiency, hygiene and the attractive decoration possible on pedestal WCs all led to the decline in demand for metal valve closets and their cabinets. Even so, Doulton retained valve closets in their 1910 bathroom catalogue.

WASH-OUT WCS

The first step towards the replacement of valve closets had been the introduction of pottery bowls. George Jennings, the Victorian sanitary engineer, collaborated with Thomas Twyford to develop a *wash-out* WC. Jennings installed early versions of his wash-out WC in the public toilets at the 1851 Great Exhibition. He patented his design the following year. Jennings's wash-out bowl featured a shallow dished tray holding an inch (25 mm) of water to prevent fouling the bowl. Progressive development of Jennings's design paved the way for important improvements in closet design.

Jennings fought hard to secure a contract for the installation of public toilets in the Great Exhibition's Crystal Palace. Records show that 827,280 visitors (14 per cent) paid to use Jennings's public toilets. There was a penny charge for using the exhibition toilets, hence the term 'spending a penny'. The penny was dropped into a

Twyford one-piece wash-out WC decorated for free-standing installation without the traditional wooden cabinet. Cleaning the voids between bowl and trap was an unpleasant task.

Jennings's combined WC and urinal with tip-up seat for female public toilets.

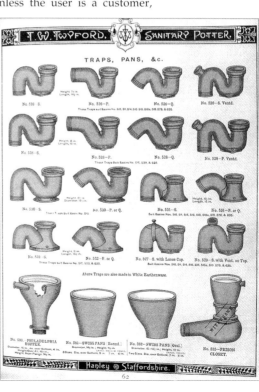

door-mounted slot machine to unlock the WC compartment for the user, providing complete privacy. There was no charge for men wishing to use the urinals. After the Great Exhibition closed the Crystal Palace was re-erected at Sydenham, in South London, where Jennings earned £1000 a year from the visitors' toilets he installed at the new site. Jennings offered to install and staff other public conveniences, or 'halting stations' as he called them, free of charge, provided he was allowed to receive a small fee for their use. London's first 'gents' public toilets were opened in Fleet Street in 1851, followed in 1852 by a 'ladies' toilet at 51 Bedford Street, Strand. The penny charge differential between genders remained until 1990 when British main-line railway stations charged everyone 20p for entrance to their toilet areas. Motorway service stations, urban public toilets and most department stores no longer charge for the use of clean toilets and washing facilities. One exception is a London store which, unless the user is a customer, charges men and women one pound a visit.

Thomas Twyford set himself the objective of developing a free-standing pedestal WC using the wash-out principle. Twyford and his son, Thomas William Twyford (1849–1921), worked together to create a WC with an integral

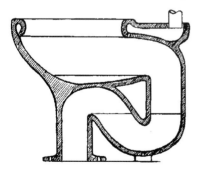

Above: *Section of Jennings's 1852 wash-out closet showing the shallow tray washed backwards into the trap with front bottom outlet.*

Right: *A page from Twyford's 1883 catalogue showing WC traps.*

Left: *Thomas William Twyford, 1849–1921, the leading sanitary potter of his day.*

Below: *Typical section of a wash-out WC: flushing water swept across the bowl into the trap.*

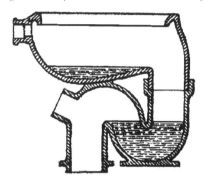

Below: *Twyford's stoneware two-piece Unitas wash-out WC with turnover rimmed bowl supported by the water-sealed trap.*

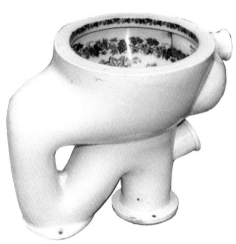

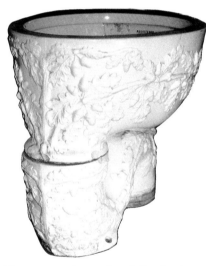

Above: *Typical early one-piece wash-out WC, a more hygienic development of plug closets, but neither type was acceptable outside a cabinet.*

bowl and trap contained inside a supporting pedestal. By the time of his early death in 1872 Thomas Twyford had helped to make substantial progress in the development of one-piece pedestal WCs. Thomas William Twyford, at the age of twenty-three, replaced his father in running the company. Young Twyford soon equalled his father's capabilities as a ceramic sanitary engineer, overcoming the making and firing problems associated with one-piece WCs.

The flushing action of Jennings's wash-out WC had directed water towards the front, washing the tray's contents backwards over a weir into the trap. To harness the water's full power, Twyford reversed the

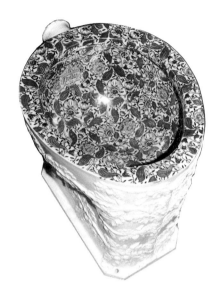

Above left: *Unitas patented one-piece wash-out WC with the trappage and bowl supported and enclosed inside the supporting pedestal, thus overcoming the cleaning problem. Pedestals provided an ideal area for decoration, in this case raised acorns and oak leaves around the outside with blue transfers inside the bowl.*

Above right: *The integral spreader plate under the back rim directs a screen of water to sweep the tray's contents forwards into and through the trap.*

Left: *WCs on unventilated sewer systems could have their seals syphoned away by turbulence in the drains. The after-flush chamber continued to drain after the flush to refill the shallow tray and reseal the trap.*

flushing direction and outlet configuration of Jennings's wash-out bowl and trap. Twyford directed the flush from the back across the tray, over a front weir into the trap. The first development stage involved attaching the bowl and trap during production. Initial attempts left voids around and beneath the bowl and trap. The final stage was to conceal the trap formation within an integral pedestal. As a result of these developments Twyford was able to introduce in 1883 the first pedestal WC to be made in one piece – the *Unitas*.

Early closets had incorporated copper spreader plates to form a water screen for cleansing the bowl. Twyford perfected the wash-out WC's flushing efficiency with an integral pottery spreader to replace the copper plate. The spreader cleared the tray whilst water flushed

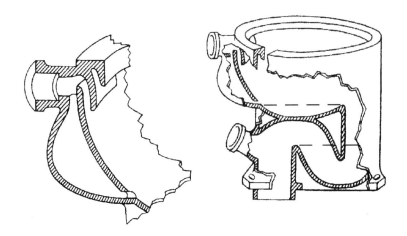

On the left, a section through the Unitas wash-out pedestal WC's after-flush chamber shows the drain hole through which water drains to fill the shallow tray. The full section on the right shows how water is retained behind the weir, in the tray, to reduce fouling.

around the rim forming a front cascade to clear the trap's contents. An integral after-flush chamber, positioned behind the bowl, retained a water reservoir that drained after completion of the flush to fill the tray and reseal the trap. Twyford's Unitas proved to be the most successful free-standing, wash-out pedestal WC. He patented the innovative features of the Unitas, the *flushing rim spreader* and after-flush chamber. The closet's attractive appearance plus these patented attributes gave Twyford an operational advantage over his competitors.

The case for exposed WCs was helped further in 1886 when Queen Victoria used a Unitas WC at the Angel Hotel in Doncaster. Queen Victoria's husband, Prince Albert, had died from typhoid in 1861, and their son almost died from the same disease in October 1871. The effect of typhoid fever in the royal household helped to generate national appreciation of the need for good sanitation. Royal approval was given with the installation of Unitas WCs at Buckingham Palace. Free-standing pedestal WCs became popular in Victorian bathrooms. Victoria's patronage of WCs had a greater effect than her predecessor Queen Elizabeth I's Ajax installation at Richmond.

Pedestal WCs became accepted in free-standing form and gained a major market share to the exclusion of valve closets. The complexity of one-piece WC production differed in concept and technology from domestic pottery. The larger WCs required new skills in potting and firing that led to specialisation. By the late nineteenth century potters such as Doulton, Howson, Edward Johns, Johnson Brothers, Shanks and Twyford all had factories dedicated to the production of ceramic sanitary appliances. Royal patronage stimulated sales of pedestal WCs. Within two years of its launch the Unitas outsold competitors in volumes reaching over ten thousand WCs a year. Before the century's end, T. W. Twyford was granted a 'Royal Warrant of Appointment as Bathroom

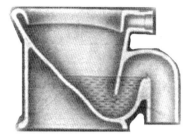

Left: *Full-front wash-down pedestal first introduced with one-piece wash-out WCs to enclose the trappage.* Right: *Wash-down WCs had no need for a trap shield at the front, thus allowing a cut-away front foot.*

and Washroom Manufacturer to Her Majesty Queen Victoria's Government'. The wash-out closet was adopted and remained the standard-type WC throughout continental Europe until the 1980s and is still popular in South America.

WASH-DOWN WCS

In 1884 Frederick Humperson introduced the wash-down WC, considered to be the first of its type. D. T. Bostel of Brighton also claimed a similar invention in 1889. Both firms had co-operated with sanitary potters and no doubt all parties contributed to the wash-down closet's development. Wash-down closets were an evolutionary development of earlier cottage pan and trap arrangements, but in one piece with the water seal raised to within the bowl. Successful operation of wash-down WCs depends on the force of flushing water to drive soil from the bowl. Early wash-downs were made with *full-front pedestals,* but later models were modified into the easier-to-make *cut-away styling.* Since 1890 the wash-down flushing principle has been adopted as the prototype for most WC development. Exported around the world, British WCs were acclaimed for their efficiency and quality, with patterns designed to suit local customs and religious needs.

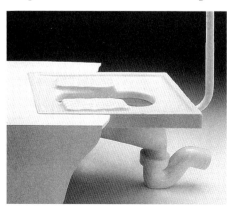

This illustration shows how squatting WCs are recessed into the ground. The pattern comprises three separate pottery elements: the fireclay top plate has foot pads and is fitted level with the finished floor; the vitreous china pan with flushing rim and separate U-bend trap fits underneath.

Ceramic materials used for WC production

Early pottery WC bowls were normally made from the same earthenware paste used for domestic utensils. Fired earthenware bodies were a creamy white colour and slightly porous. When dipped into liquid glaze and refired, earthenware acquired an impervious surface. Pottery WC bowls had easy-to-clean glazed surfaces, whereas cast-iron bowls rusted through their painted finish. Pottery's light body colour was hygienic and a visual improvement over the painted cast-iron bowls they had replaced. The transition to free-standing pottery WCs was slow.

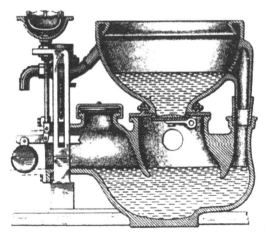

With the development of integral supporting traps WCs became more complex. These larger items required stronger construction to resist distortion during firing. Henry Doulton replaced the metal discharge chamber of his valve closet with a strong stoneware drainpipe body. Doulton originally bought white earthenware bowls from North Staffordshire for his metal valve closet combinations. These closets were successful, but Doulton wanted to make free-standing WCs and believed his impervious stoneware was an ideal material.

Stoneware was cheaper and stronger than earthenware, which convinced Henry Doulton of the material's viability. Stoneware had an impervious body and a natural matt sheen or salt-glazed glossy surface with only one firing, compared with earthenware's two. In addition stoneware had the advantage of being waterproof throughout the trappage. The disadvantage was that stoneware's brownish body showed through the transparent finish and

Doulton Lambeth valve closet with earthenware bowl and stoneware trap.

proved unpopular. The fired colour of stoneware depended on the iron oxides in local clay. The outside colour should not have concerned Victorians because most WCs, including pottery cottage types, remained hidden in cabinets. In the hope of making free-standing stoneware WCs acceptable to Victorian taste potters added decoration. Wealthy homeowners, however, had become accustomed to white glazed earthenware surfaces on the visible areas of closet bowls. Potential customers for WCs associated stoneware's brown salt-glazed surfaces with drainpipes. Stoneware's cream or brown colour proved an

Left: *1898 Doulton salt-glaze stoneware wash-out WC with raised decoration hand-painted in blue and green, on display at the Potteries Museum and Art Gallery.*

Right: *Matt sheen stoneware wash-down WC with raised decoration hand-painted in blue.*

Left: *Stoneware wash-down WC with cut-away pedestal showing the body colour through the clear glaze. Sanitary pottery with a finish like this is known as cane-and-white ware.*

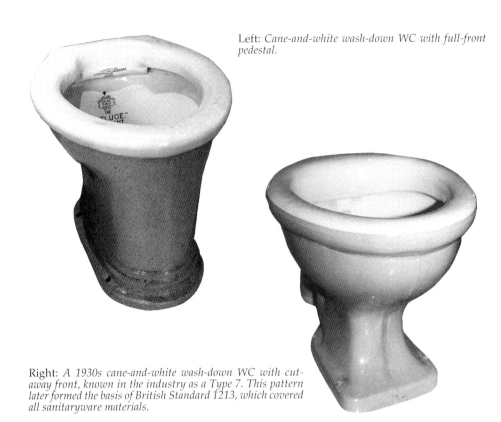

Left: *Cane-and-white wash-down WC with full-front pedestal.*

Right: *A 1930s cane-and-white wash-down WC with cut-away front, known in the industry as a Type 7. This pattern later formed the basis of British Standard 1213, which covered all sanitaryware materials.*

unpopular alternative to mahogany bathroom decor, with resultant low sales. To overcome these problems and to retain the benefits of stoneware's strong and impervious body, the buff-coloured bowl's inner surface and rim were coated with liquid white earthenware. This white surface was fused to the stoneware body in a first firing before dipping into liquid glaze and refiring. These WCs were known as *cane-and-white ware,* buff-coloured outside with white inside and on the rim. Cane-and-white became the main material for WC production in the mid nineteenth century. Impervious *vitreous china*, which was first introduced in the 1930s, replaced both cane-and-white and earthenware in the 1950s as the main material for sanitaryware production.

Decoration

Potters added decoration to stoneware bowls in an attempt to make them more attractive. Moreover, the development of one-piece pedestal WCs provided simplified shapes well suited to exterior relief or transfer decoration. Many combinations of ceramic decoration were applied to the new free-standing WCs. The pottery process enabled the pressing of various raised decorative motifs into the full-front pedestal WCs.

Transfer decoration inside early-nineteenth-century pottery valve closet bowls had already proved popular. The new pedestal WCs provided ideal surfaces for the same decorative process. Single-colour, hot-printed transfers from engraved copper plates were used on sanitaryware. Engraving was a skilled and expensive process. Transfers were often adapted for use on several designs to spread the engraving cost.

Transfers and raised decorations were also used as painting guides

A selection of raised decoration on full-front-pedestal wash-out and wash-down WC basins: (above, from left to right) Deluge, Deluge, Oracle; (below, from left to right) Royal, Dolphin, Darrah.

A selection of decoration by hot-pressed transfers from copper plates on full-front-pedestal wash-out and wash-down WCs: (top row, left to right) Doulton, Combination, Ricardia; (middle row) Shanks Junction, viewed from two angles; (bottom row) Latestas, cut-away style.

Above left: *Shanks Citizen WC with hand-painted exterior and interior bowl decoration.*

Above right: *Twyford Twycliffe WC with hand-enamelled raised exterior decoration.*

Right: *Ideal-Standard Neoline WC with matching seat and bidet.*

Below left: *A typical Victorian catalogue page showing the choice of decoration on the Twycliffe.*

Below right: *Illustration from Doulton's 1910 catalogue, captioned: 'Improved valve closet is strongly recommended for high-class work'.*

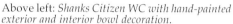

Designs of the "Twycliffe" Patent Syphon Closet Basin.

Left: *Doulton's 1912 WC with raised Art Nouveau decoration on pedestal and bowl.*

Right: *Twyford's 1929 Trident bulbous syphonic WC suite with cut-corner styling.*

in the more expensive process of hand-colouring. Readily available in Staffordshire was expertise in hand-painting, copper-plate engraving and transfer-printing. Victorian catalogues show that most WCs were available with a wide choice of decoration.

Throughout their short history sanitary pottery designs have embraced many decorative styles to satisfy ever changing fashion and taste. By the start of the twentieth century the ornate and colourful decoration popular during Queen Victoria's reign waned as Art Nouveau's sinuous plant forms appeared on WC pedestals. By 1920 the highly colourful Victorian transfer and painted ornamentation had been rejected in favour of plain white – white bathrooms became commonplace in many new council houses and most middle-class homes. The Art Deco styles of the 1920s came and went and most forms of applied decoration disappeared in favour of Modernist styling.

The Modernist influence of Art Deco sharpened the soft lines of WC designs. Cut corners and straight sides replaced curves and round edges. Wealthy householders, keen to rise above the level of the working classes, demanded coloured sanitaryware, introduced in 1925. The cost of producing coloured ware was spread over smaller quantities than the white output, resulting in higher prices being charged. Coloured ware was priced beyond the reach of lower-paid workers and some middle-class buyers. Art Deco trends briefly popularised black and peony sanitaryware, but European and North American markets preferred the pastel colours of turquoise, lavender, primrose, blue, pink and ivory.

Flushing efficiency, syphonic and close-coupled WCs

The availability of piped water in the eighteenth century made it possible to install and fill roof-space storage tanks serving upper floors. These water reservoirs at constant pressure made possible the installation of high-level cisterns connected to water closets by a flushpipe. High-level cisterns fitted at 2 metres controlled the force of flushing water and replaced supply valves for flushing WCs. To utilise the kinetic energy of cleansing water effectively and to contain spillage, WCs were made with full or box flushing rims.

Pulling the chain operated a *cistern flushing valve* mechanism on early high-level cisterns. This action raised a plug outlet in the cistern to discharge water into the flushpipe. Grit and lime soon built up on outlet seatings, making the flush less effective and eventually causing wastage. Householders also abused cistern fittings by securing the pull chain to leave the outlet valve open, allowing a constant trickle of water intended to keep WCs fresh and clean. This abuse led to substantial wastage of the meagre water supplies.

Section through a valveless waste-preventing syphon to explain the operation, displayed at the Science Museum, London.

The problems of water wastage were overcome in the late 1870s by the development of the valveless syphon to replace the leakage-prone valve flushing units. Valveless syphons were operated by similar pull-and-let-go chains. The pull action lifted a piston-type diaphragm forcing water over the syphon invert to start the flush. Water pours down the flushpipe, drawing the cistern's water contents behind it into the WC. When the cistern's water level dropped below the syphon base, air entered to stop the syphonic action. Syphons had no valve to leave open, so the cistern could not be operated again until it refilled. It was no use holding down the chain as no more water could be flushed from the cistern until it refilled.

Many plumbing engineers contributed towards the successful development of the *valveless water waste preventing* (WWP) *syphon*.

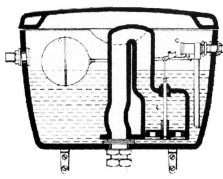

Section through a valveless flushing syphon. Water lifted in the bell charges the up-leg and flows over the syphon invert to start the syphon's operation. When the water level falls below the bell's base, air intake stops the flush.

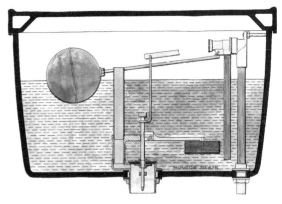

Above: *Pulling the valve cistern chain lifted an outlet valve from its seating to release the flush. The falling water level lowers the valve, closing the outlet to refill the cistern.*

Left: *High-level WC illustrated in T. W. Twyford's 1898 'Twentieth Century Catalogue'.*

Right: *Victorian high-level WC with cast-iron cistern and flushpipe encased in mahogany.*

Doulton, Edward Johns, Shanks and Twyfords all catalogued water waste preventing syphons. Thomas Crapper was only one amongst many plumbers who installed valveless syphons, but he was not the inventor. The valveless syphon provided a constant and repeatable flushing control that helped potters to further improve WC flushing efficiency. Cisterns were gradually lowered, but many remained in mahogany casings, often extended into WC seats and covers. Hinged wooden seats for pedestal WCs were secured to the wall or floor on cast-iron brackets or wooden frames. Seats were independent of, but rested on, floor-mounted closets. In 1911 WC basins were first made with lug holes so that the seat could be attached directly.

The flushing actions of wash-out and wash-down WCs depended on water driving the bowl's contents through the trappage. Several inventors concentrated on evacuation by using the syphonic principle to clear WCs. Syphonic WCs rely on the creation of a partial vacuum, or water build-up within the trappage, to pull sewage through to the drain.

The profits from his public toilets installed at the Great Exhibition helped George Jennings finance work on syphonic WCs. Jennings's syphonic 'Closet of the Century' won a gold medal at the 1884 International Health Exhibition at South Kensington. Most of the

Above left: *WC seat and cover supported on cast-iron floor brackets. Access to the trap joint was gained by removing loose plates in the foot.*

Above right: *To flush WCs efficiently at lower levels, the Victorians used large, 3 gallon (13.6 litre) cast-iron cisterns with large-bore flushpipes encased in mahogany extended into seat assemblies.*

flushing water discharged directly into a separate second trap below the floor level. This action induced air displacement to pull the bowl's contents from the WC's first trap. The syphonic action of Jennings's Closet of the Century used a lot of water and the complicated pipework

Left: *Jennings's syphonic 'Closet of the Century'.*

Below right: *Section of Jennings's syphonic closet showing the single trap within the basin and a second trap below floor level.*

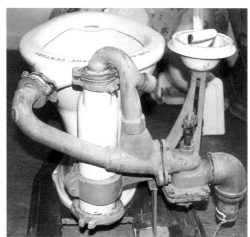

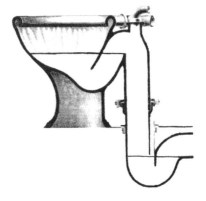

Twycliffe syphon-jet closet with pressed-in raised decoration being made on a potter's workshop bench at Twyford's Cliffe Vale factory in 1898.

and unsightly valve apparatus had to be concealed in a cabinet. Both of these characteristics were contrary to the potters' objective of developing free-standing WCs that used the minimum of water.

SINGLE-TRAP SYPHONIC WCS

Equally effective but less complex syphonic-action WCs soon replaced Jennings's invention. Thomas Twyford's potting expertise enabled him to condense Jennings's spaghetti of pipes into two integral flushing channels on the Twycliffe syphonic WC. The twin jet streams flushed

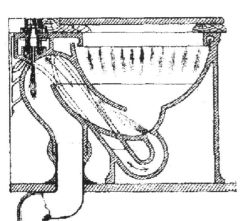

into the WC sump below the water level and down into the outlet, inducing a syphon by displacement. The combined action of drive and pull cleansed the bowl and cleared the sump of soiled matter. WCs with the Twycliffe action became known as 'syphon-jet' types. Although syphon-jet WCs are no longer made in Britain they remain a feature of American sanitaryware.

British inventors developed other

Early Twycliffe WCs had twin jets to create a syphonic action. The main jet entered below water level to drive the sump's contents into the trap. A second jet was directed from the flushpipe to the trap's down-leg, pushing waste into the drain.

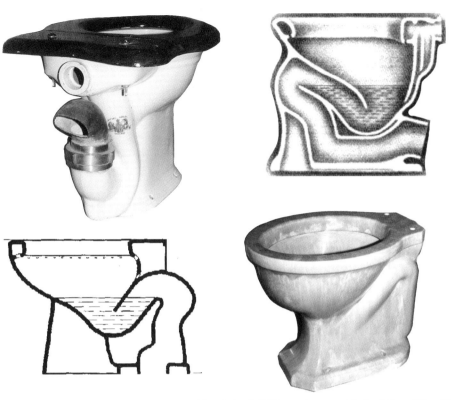

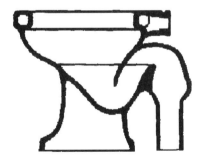

Top left: *A 1912 royal warrant badged Twycliffe with a single water-jet chamber directed part of the flush into the trap's up-leg.*

Top right: *Wash-down syphonic WC with convoluted trappage.*

Centre left: *Bottom-outlet wash-down syphonic WC with zigzag trappage to retard the flow and form a liquid vortex to generate a syphonic action.*

Centre right: *Bottom-outlet syphonic WCs were used with the underfloor plumbing common in America.*

Left: *The bulbous trap wash-down syphonic WC depends on narrowing the trap bore to retard the flow and form a syphonic plug to draw the contents from the bowl.*

efficient methods of WC clearance based on syphonic actions, making partial use of the wash-down operating principle. Instead of a full-bore trappage, the basin outflow was slowed by trap distortion or restriction. A syphonic action was created when the retarded flow of water and soil in the trap built up to form a temporary liquid vortex within the bowl. The gravitational pull from the fully charged trappage, helped by atmospheric pressure on the water area within the bowl, forced out the basin contents. These WC types are variously known as *single-trap*

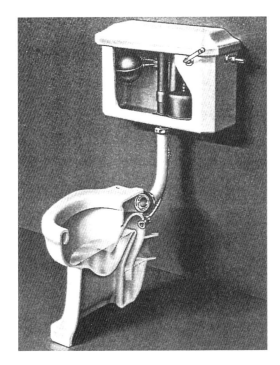

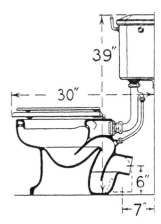

Above: *A sectional detail of a double-trap syphonic WC showing the water levels and air pipe inlet.*

Left: *A catalogue illustration explaining to potential buyers the operation of a double-trap syphonic WC and low-level cistern with separate pipe to extract air from between the two traps.*

syphonic, or in the United States *reverse trap* or *wash-down syphonic.* Variants of these single-trap syphonic WCs are still in production today, but the reduced bores of their trappages are prone to blockage if misused.

DOUBLE-TRAP SYPHONIC WCS

By the early 1900s the introduction of syphonic closets made possible the use of low-level flushing cisterns, fitted below a metre in overall height. According to a 1920s catalogue the flush of low-level double-trap syphonic WC suites was 'practically inaudible outside the compartment'. An 'extra large water area' prevented fouling of the bowl's sides. Double-trap syphonic WCs incorporate Jennings's idea of reducing air pressure between water-sealed traps. Unlike Jennings's design, later double-trap syphonic WCs used the whole volume of flushed water to cleanse the bowl, eject its contents and reseal both traps. In the 1930s improvements in the production process enabled potters to incorporate the twin traps within the closet's pedestal. Because the syphonic effect operates throughout the flush, double-trap WCs are termed *continuous action syphonics.*

Early double-trap syphonic WCs operated under low-level cisterns delivering water through a flushpipe that incorporated an internal hood restriction. Water flowing down the restricted flushpipe created an air-pressure differential, pulling air through a pipe connected to a space between traps. This action, caused by a *Venturi* effect, creates a

Left: *This type of bottom-outlet syphonic WC for the American market, with 3 gallon (13.6 litre) valve-flushing cisterns, made possible the first close-coupled WC suites.*

Right: *Detail of the totally enclosed Venturi pressure-reducing fitting connected to the air space void between the traps of the close-coupled double-trap syphonic suites shown below.*

Below left: *Twyford's 1939 Unitas-Silent close-coupled double-trap syphonic WC suite with colour-matched plastic seat and cover. When first introduced, these suites were fitted with mahogany seat and covers.*

Below right: *A 1950s Brampton close-coupled double-trap syphonic WC suite, originally fitted with a matching sky-blue plastic seat and cover. In 1999 a wooden seat replaced the coloured plastic seat, reflecting the late-twentieth-century taste for natural materials.*

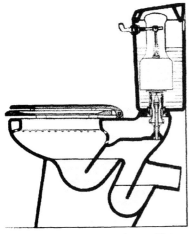

Section of a close-coupled double-trap syphonic WC suite showing the two traps within the supporting pedestal foot.

powerful suction of air from between the traps. The resultant partial vacuum draws the bowl's contents from the first trap into the drainage system. The Venturi effect created in double-trap syphonic WCs is the same principle that draws air into the carburettor of an internal combustion petrol engine.

In 1966 *The Lancet* medical journal praised double-trap syphonic WC suites for their negligible dispersal of bacterial aerosol during flushing. This feature satisfied the growing awareness of health and safety in the home. Double-trap syphonic WCs have the unique efficiency of economic use of water, quietness in operation and an hygienic action with virtually no associated aerosol spray.

CLOSE-COUPLED WC SUITES

The American-type wash-down syphonic closets enabled 3 gallon (13.6 litre) cisterns with valve flushing units to be bolted directly on to WCs as *close-coupled suites*. However, close-coupled double-trap syphonic WCs then required an alternative to the flushpipe-induced pressure-reduction system. In the late 1930s Victor Pimble of Twyfords patented a pressure-reducing fitment inserted between the cistern and WC basin. This bullet-shaped fitting, placed in the cistern outlet, created an even better Venturi effect than the flushpipe pattern. Twyford's double-trap syphonic suite became the industry's benchmark, but Pimble's patent protection secured a substantial long-term market lead.

Flushing technology and efficiency continued to develop until the mid 1930s, when wash-down WCs could also operate efficiently with close-coupled cisterns. By the end of the twentieth century high-level cisterns had virtually disappeared. Close-coupled wash-down WC suites became a European standard in the 1980s. American-influenced markets prefer syphonic types and allow water at mains pressure directly into WC sumps, on the syphon-jet principle.

In the 1950s vacuum WCs were widely used on ships, but the noisy flush action made them unpopular in domestic situations. Pressurised WC flushing systems were an American development during the 1980s. This system works on the principle that air has elasticity, allowing it to be compressed. Water cannot be compressed: if it is squeezed, it squirts. American mains water pressure is harnessed to compress air within a WC cistern's sealed tank. Flushing the cistern releases the compressed air, forcing water and bowl contents into the drain. Foul water is prevented from backflowing into mains supplies. To protect water purity, the American system is not allowed in European homes.

WCs in the third millennium

Victorian sanitary potters and engineers made outstanding contributions to public health with the development of the water-sealed trap WC. This was a major factor in beating cholera. Since the middle of the eighteenth century efficient WCs have become available to all social classes in most of the world's developed countries. When eighteenth-century British potters replaced metal valve closets with pottery bowls they created what became a worldwide industry. Sanitaryware manufacturers have received royal approval. Thomas William Twyford's company received recognition with a royal warrant for his contribution to WC design. Henry Doulton was knighted by Queen Victoria in 1887, the first potter to receive the accolade, and Edward VII awarded him a royal warrant for the company's contribution to sanitary science. Permission was given in 1901 to call the company Royal Doulton. Edward VII granted Thomas Crapper a royal warrant; George V made a similar appointment to Ideal-Standard. On the 150th anniversary of his birth, T. W. Twyford would have felt justifiably proud that in 1999 his family company was granted the 'Royal Warrant of Appointment as Manufacturers of Bathroom and Washroom Fittings to Her Majesty Queen Elizabeth II'.

What fashion trends, design styles and technical innovations can we expect in the third millennium? Production methods and materials have improved, but since the Second World War there have been virtually no innovative changes to WC operation methods. One could claim that the operational methods developed so long ago need no improvement. Even the electronic cleansing facilities provided with combined WC and bidet for the severely disabled depend on the wash-down principle to clear soil. Improved WC efficiency paved the way for European legislation to reduce cistern flushing capacities from 9 to 6 litres. However, existing house drains require adequate hydraulic flow to maintain their self-cleansing systems. What effect reduced flushing capacities will have on clearance of existing drains is open to question.

From 2001 European Community rules will allow the reintroduction of continental-type cistern flushing valves in Britain. This will bring the advantage of a button-operated flush rather than a lever. Experience will show whether cistern outlet leakage problems, caused by lime deposit, have been cured on the new valves. Victorians banned flushing valves because they leaked and wasted water, whereas continental WC flushing valves continue to leak.

Nostalgic Victorian- and Edwardian-style bathrooms were popular for the last two decades of the twentieth century. Over 30 per cent of showroom displays in 2000 retained some Victorian styles. Although WC quality, clearance and outlet joints are far superior to Victorian standards, many modern designs copy Victorian fashions. It is to be hoped that British designers can create some new, progressive styling early in the third millennium.

Left: *Six-litre push-button Entice WC suite with dual flush option, c.2000.*

WCs showing the styles popular from the 1960s to the 1990s: (above) 1964 school WC; (centre left) 1970s; (centre right) 1980s; (bottom left) 1987; (bottom right) 1994, Italian.

Left: *1979 Victorian-style set.*

Below: *1999 Victorian-style high-level wash-down WC. The exposed flushpipe and wooden seat and cover add a degree of authenticity.*

Left: *1999 Victorian-style wash-down WC, but cisterns were first bolted directly on to basins as close-coupled suites in the 1930s, long after Victorian times.*

Glossary

Ajax: Sir John Harington's WC, a corruption of the Elizabethan term 'a jakes' describing a privy.

Bourdalou: a urinary pot for women. Also called a coach or carriage pot. Name attributed to Père Louis Bourdaloue, a popular Jesuit preacher who served in Louis XIV's court.

Box, full or returned flushing rims: rims on WCs were first returned, then turned down into the bowl, then boxed in.

Bramah, Joseph: the second person to patent a WC, this with a hinged outlet valve.

Cane-and-white ware: WCs made from a blend of ball and china clays with Cornish stone, white earthenware coated inside and on the rim, fired to a cream colour, then refired with a clear glaze.

Cistern flushing valve: WC cistern outlet mechanism, liable to water wastage.

Close-coupled suite: a WC with a cistern bolted directly to the basin.

Close stool water closet: an early type of WC made by Wedgwood.

Continuous action syphonic: the double-trap pattern, which pulls the bowl's contents throughout the flush.

Cottage pan: a type of simple pan WC with a bowl or pan and separate trap.

A page from a Twyford 1910 catalogue captioned 'A Modern Bathroom'.

Cummings, Alexander: a watchmaker from Bond Street, London, who patented the first WC in 1775.

Cut-away styling: wash-down WC with a recessed front.

Doulton, Henry: manufacturer of sanitaryware and stoneware drainpipes which helped eliminate cholera from Victorian London.

Flushing rim spreader: an integral clay plate fixed under the rim to form a screen of water to wash the contents of the WC tray into the trap.

Full flushing rims: see **Box flushing rims**.

Full-front pedestal: WC with the trap formation concealed by an integral skirting.

Jennings, George: Victorian sanitary engineer, inventor and pioneer promoter of public toilets.

Liverpool pan: a type of simple WC with a bowl or pan and separate trap.

Plunger or plug closet: an early one-piece pottery WC.

Privy: an ashpit or pail closet from which waste matter was emptied manually.

Returned flushing rims: see **Box flushing rims**.

Reverse-trap/single-trap/wash-down syphonic: WC basin with restricted trap to induce a syphonic action.

Spigot: an integral hollow pottery tube to supply water to or act as an overflow for a WC.

Stink-trap: patented by John Gaittait in 1782, to prevent cesspit gases entering dwellings.

Syphon-jet: a WC in which some flushing water is directed into the trappage, creating a jet stream to pull soil from the sump.

Twyford, Thomas: manufacturer of sanitaryware; collaborated with Jennings to develop the wash-out WC.

Twyford, Thomas William: son of Thomas Twyford; developed the first pedestal WC.

U-bend: a U-shaped tubular form filled with water to create a seal against cesspit or sewer gas.

Unitas: wash-out WC made by Thomas William Twyford.

Valve closet: early WC with a metal valve outlet.

Valveless water waste preventing syphon: introduced to discharge flushing water into WCs, to overcome water wastage through leakage from valve-type flushing systems.

Venturi: a device using fluid flow over a constricted opening causing suction of air to create pressure differential, as in a carburettor air inlet.

Vitreous china: a dense, impervious white pottery used in the manufacture of sanitary pottery.

Wash-down WC: a basin with controlled flush meeting at the bowl front and directing the flow on to the water area, driving soil through the full-bore water-sealed trap.

Wash-out WC: developed by George Jennings and Thomas Twyford; water is directed across a shallow tray to wash the contents over a weir into the trap.

Watercock: early term for water-supply control valves or taps.

Water-sealed trap: U-shaped formation full of water to prevent cesspit gas escaping through the WC.

Further reading

Blair, Munroe. *Now Wash Your Hands: Ablutionary Ceramics.* In preparation during 2000.
Evamy, M. *The First Hundred Years.* Ideal-Standard, 1996.
Eyles, D. *Sanitation through the Ages.* Official Architect, 1941.
Lambton, L. *Temples of Convenience and Chambers of Delight.* Pavilion Books, 1995.
Reyburn, W. *Flushed with Pride.* Pavilion Books, 1989.
Wedd, K. *The Victorian Bathroom Catalogue.* Studio Editions, 1996.
Wood, R. *Loos through the Ages.* Batsford, 1986. (For children.)
Wright, L. *Clean and Decent.* Routledge & Kegan Paul, 1960.

Places to visit

To ensure the items you want to see are on display, it is recommended that interested visitors telephone before travelling.

Abbey Pumping Station Museum, Corporation Road, Leicester LE4 5PX. Telephone: 0116 299 5111. Website: www.leicestermuseums.ac.uk

The Crossness Engines Trust, Thames Water Crossness Works, Belvedere Road, Abbey Wood, London SE2 9AQ. Telephone enquiries: 020 8303 6723. (Visits by appointment.)

Gladstone Working Pottery Museum, Uttoxeter Road, Longton, Stoke-on-Trent ST3 1PQ. Telephone: 01782 319232 or 311378. Website: www.stoke.gov.uk/gladstone (The Ceramic Sanitaryware Gallery of this working museum reopens in summer 2001, after refurbishment, to house one of the most comprehensive displays of historic WCs in Britain.)

Museum of Science and Industry in Manchester, Liverpool Road, Castlefield, Manchester M3 4FP. Telephone: 0161 832 2244. Website: www.edes.co.uk/mussci

Newarke Houses Museum, The Newarke, Leicester LE2 7BY. Telephone: 0116 247 3222.

Science Museum, Exhibition Road, South Kensington, London SW7 2DD. Telephone: 020 7942 4214. Website: www.sciencemuseum.org.uk (Selection of WCs and associated drainpipes.)

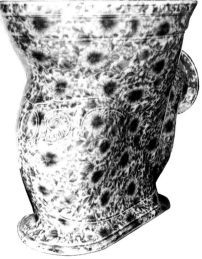

The Empire, a full-front-pedestal wash-out basin with transfer and raised decoration.